INTRODUCTION

In this, my nineteenth book in the "Around" series, I have returned to South Gloucestershire and in particular to the substantially developed area just north of Bristol that over the past sixty years or so has grown beyond all recognition from the small communities that were once self-sufficient in Winterbourn Down; Winterbourne, Frampton Cotterell, and Iron Acton. Within this book the pictorial journey start at Pye Corner where my book *Around Downend, Frenchay & Hambrook* stopped, and at that point we immediately run into the controversy of an 'E' or no 'E' and as can be seen above Winterbourn Down under the Order in Council of the 25th July 1861 does not have the final 'E', whilst Winterbourne including the Civil Parish does, but despite that Order so often the extra 'E' is misused. Almost certainly the earliest human settlement in the area covered by the book occurred during the Stone Age when Iberians roamed the hills and valleys and may well have buried their dead under the large mound at Hill Crest, and defended themselves at places such as Bury Hill. By the end of the first century most of the land in and around the three settlements had fallen to the might of the Roman Legions, although with little or no bloodshed as many of the local Celts either joined the Legions, or farmed the fertile soil and raised food, particularly wheat for export to other parts of the Empire. This arrangement lasted for around four hundred years, and then the Romans left leaving a void until the seventh century when the Anglo-Saxons arrived. Exactly when Winterbourne was named is not known but it is recorded in the Domesday Book as Wintreborne, meaning a winter stream, a place where the stream only flows during the winter months. Frampton can be identified as the settlement that straddles the R. Frome, but probably did not develop until the fifth/six century as even by the mid part of the eleventh century there were only twenty householders or around 125 persons. During the following century the Cotele family held the local manor, and it was from their surname that the middle village epithet was derived. Part of the extensive Kingswood Forest the whole area was inhabited to work the fertile land, creating over many centuries a very rustic group of small hamlets, but a reasonable sized industrial heritage began during the eighteenth century starting with quarrying, hat making; coal mining and the extraction of iron ore causing a substantial growth in the population and the gradual merger of the hamlets into villages that continued to grow. However, in a more modest way iron ore was found amongst the oak trees in Saxon time leading to the establishment of Iron Acton.

The preparation of this book would not have been possible without the help of David Williams who kindly directed me in the right direction to identify the position of some of the old photographs: Sheila Brooks for reading and correcting the transcript, Derek and Janet Fisher and Mike Tozer for allowing me to use some of their pictures. At all times I have endeavoured to minimise any mistakes made but should any exist then they are unfortunately of my own making, for which I apologise and trust that they will not distract you from enjoying the remaining contents.

August 2013 Ian S Bishop

Bristol Road winds its way through Pye Corner as it dips to the junction with Quarry Barton, before climbing on its way to Winterbourne. The photographer has caught the attention of a young lady and two gentlemen, but the rest of this community appear totally unconcerned that this moment in time has been frozen for ever, c1908

The old and derelict cottages that in their heyday were known as Willow Rank, Winterbourne Hill, March 1989. (for comparison see also picture on page 3)

Looking up Whiteshill from the entrance into the grounds of the *White Horse Inn* with the habited row of cottages on the left known as Willow Rank, whilst on the right somewhat hiding behind the trees is Dr Crossman's hospital, c1935. For a different perspective on this view please refer to my book "*Around Downend, Frenchay, & Hambrook.*

A c1904 view looking across the fields that having parted exposes a small section of Worrel's Lane, as it sweeps up the hill before it becomes Mill Road and then travels on towards the old rectory, and the 1866 built church school. Also visible are the rear of the cottages that make up Frome Glen.

The River Frome as it meanders its peaceful and gentle way through the valley that skirts around the eastern side of Winterbourn Down passing as it does a fisherman patiently waiting for that intense moment when the lurking fish takes the bait of a free meal and becomes one itself, c1905

The somewhat unique Moorend Mill inasmuch as it is a single storied building whereas the majority of mills are constructed with at least two stories, plus it has a very distinctive undershot waterwheel that is almost as tall as the mill itself. Almost certainly the mill was designed in this fashion solely for the purpose of being able to grind/roll blank iron bars into their required shape. It is believed that the mill was constructed around 1850 on behalf of the Frenchay Iron Co with one other unique feature being that the mill was constructed on an island in the middle of the River Frome hence the need for the visible footbridge, c1904. As the local source of iron ore began to depreciate, (over 7,000 tons per annum were dug locally in the 1860/70's) the iron workings moved to the Midlands where there was a larger source of both iron and coal, and the technology of making improved iron caused the mill to become redundant, and it soon fell into a state of disrepair as seen on the right around 1912.

With one young man perched on the wall plus two dismounted cyclists the photographer has constructed a more interesting picture of the cottage at the bottom of Mill Steps. Note the sign on the left warning carters the danger of the hill and the possibility of runaway wagons, recommending that suitable adjustments be made to the reins, c 1910

All Saints Church built 1858 in memory of the Revd Frederick Greenstreet's parents on land previously occupied by squatters as Down Road sweeps around the Winterbourn Down United Free Methodist Church, (built 1879) that is partly hidden on the right by the high wall and foliage. At first glance there is little dating evidence in this view, except that the bell tower is seen towards the front of the church rather than at the back as it is today as this did not occur until 1949, it is probable that this view is c1935. The squatters that once occupied the site were in the main unruly colliers, with a sprinkling of hatters.

More of a broadside view of All Saints church clearly showing the bell tower at the right-hand end of the building. In the middle of this view it is possible to make out the steps leading to the lower churchyard, containing on the left a large stone crucifix, which together with the steps (constructed in 1912), are memorials to the late Revd William Henderson. To the right is a more slender cross that is dedicated to two brothers one of whom fell in World War 1. With the agreement of that family, the names of other local men who did not return during two World Wars were also inscribed, c1922

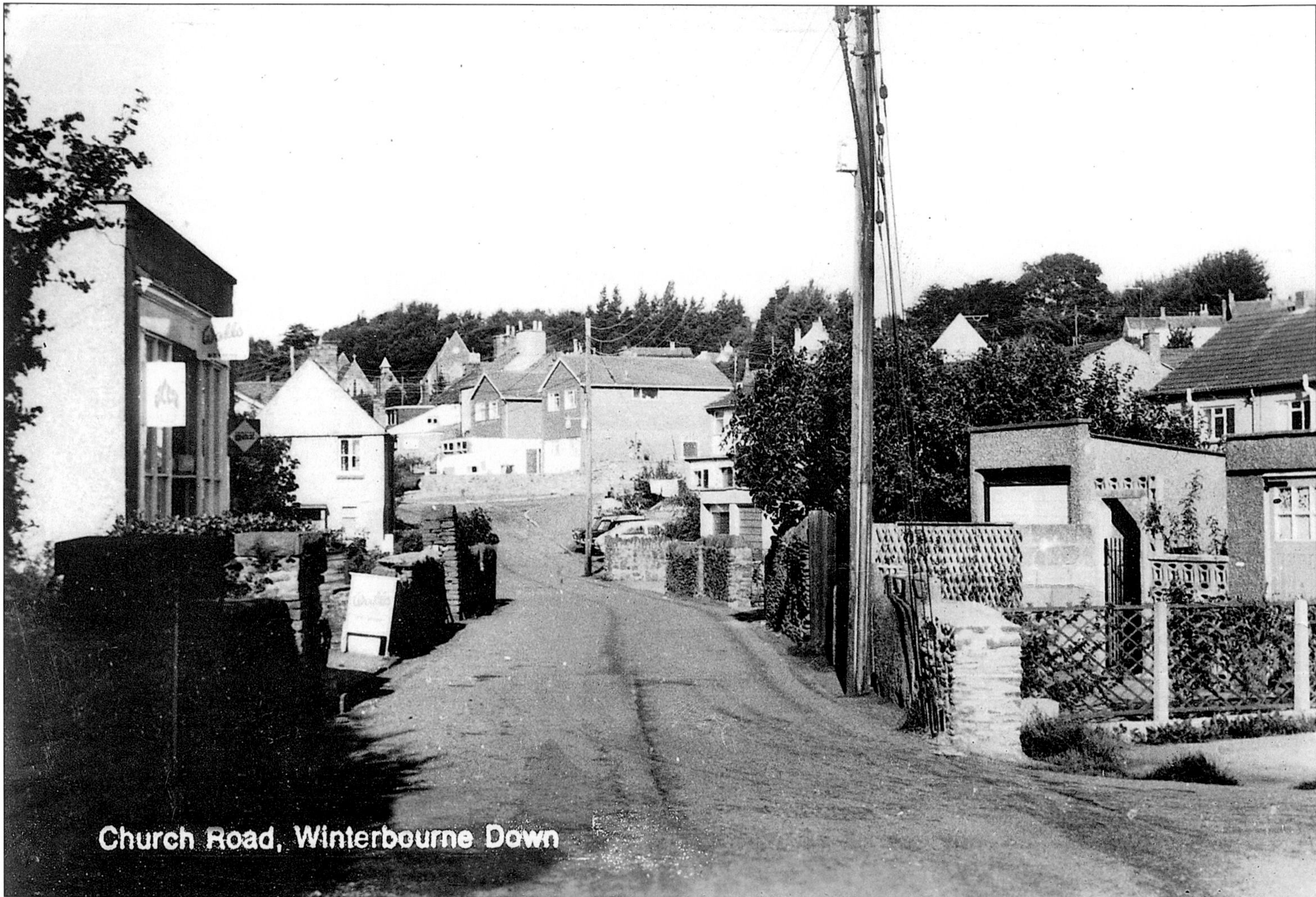

Looking along Church Road around 1960 towards All Saints, with Porter's general grocery store on the left. Previously known as DeGay's it was, before World War Two, owned and run by Robert Earnest Gay. It is believed that the shop closed in the early eighties and converted into a house.

The *Cross Hands* public house as we look along a very quiet Down Road at its junction with Church Road on the left and Harcombe Hill on the right, taken from a card sent all the way to Pennsylvania (USA), c1955.

A bevy of children have been arranged across the road by the photographer outside the *Royal Oak* and the public weighbridge by the white bag, administered from the small building in front of the inn. Behind the children is a group of men trying to be as innocuous as possible after all who wants their picture taken! as they stand outside a general store, c1904

A view of the junction of High Street with Beacon Lane as it enters on the left, and Flaxpits Lane on the right. saloon cars are parked in the forecourt of the *Royal Oak* whilst a Ford Cortina (591 FLF) approaches a mini congestion in the heat of the day, c1959.

A knife sharpener plies his trade on the side of a peaceful High Street as we look towards Watley's End. A general store selling anything from haberdashery to beer, to groceries and owned by T H Grove is on the left, whilst beyond the van is a rank of terraced cottages that were colloquially known as "Donkey Terrace" owing to the fact that the gentleman who lived in the end terrace cottage kept a donkey, c1911.

As soon as motorised transport became more reliable, it became a form of massed transport, and here we have an official photograph of Bristol Tramway's single deck bus type C65, registeration AE731 that inaugurated the country route from the Tramway Centre to Winterbourne, via Newfoundland Road; Eastville; Stapleton; Frenchay, and Hambrook, c1914

Winterbourne High Street sweeps around towards Watley's End passing "Donkey Terrace" on the left, with the old forge and general workshop on the right. Three elderly and bearded gentlemen pose for the camera to help create the evocative nature of this part of the village as it once was. The enamel sheet advertises Young & Howe furniture makers, c1902

St Michael the parish church of Winterbourne was built of stone in the Early English decorated style probably during the fourteenth century with a chancel, five bay nave, a south porch, plus tower with pinnacles, and a spire containing a clock and six bells, although part of the building can be traced back to pre-Norman time. It is understood that on at least two occasions the impressive spire has been damaged by lightning, and was last restored in 1951, ie after the date of this photograph, c1904

The above picture views the church from Court Farm (E Eden Jones ~ farmer), whilst the view on the right has been taken from Church Lane, and includes a cluster of attractive cottages and a lady just about to cycle into the village, c1927

Although built back in 1869, the pavement area leading to St Michael's school and rooms appears to be in the same condition as the builders left it. The photographer has arranged a number of children from the school; the majority of whom are wrapped up against the winter cold albeit the majority if them have sensibly stayed away from the mud and dirt, c1904

Looking along High Street and its solitary handcart, and motorcycle sidecar with the tall St Michael's school building on the right next-door to the premises from which Annie Dando ran her general store. Sadly that building together with the adjacent white buildings were demolished so that a car park could be constructed, beyond the building with the porch is *The Wheatsheaf* public house, picture c1910.

The photographer must have spent some while organising and arranging the composition of this interesting picture. Four young smartly dressed girls have been strategically placed at the front with groups of other children and adults scattered behind them. On the right a gentlemen, ~ possibly the local doctor, ~ lounges over his trap, an elderly lady tentatively looks out from the safety of her house, whilst the landlord of *The Wheatsheaf* public house watches over the proceedings; although the local dog, disturbed from his slumbers, is not sure what all the commotion is about, c1904

The High Street continues on its way towards Watley's End past ranks of cottages on both side intermingled with more substantial villas. On the left at the far end of the rank are the premises of a newly fledged business about to be started by Alex Jones, whilst the rank on the right includes Daniel Elliott's grocery shop, c1904

Below the angle of the camera has been changed to a more interesting view and the cameraman has succeeded in gathering a large group of children from the village including three young ladies kitted out in their Sunday best, plus a young man in a sailor suit, and three slightly older boys complete with their Eton collars. In the background a large farm wagon complete with a substantial load of hay helps to give us a small glimpse of village life one hundred year's ago, c1906

With the camera pulled back we are in this picture allowed to see *The Grove* a substantial house occupied by Daniel Matthews and his family, including his son Harry Grindle Matthews (1880-1941). For many people particularly the modern generation Harry's name will have no significance, but during his lifetime he was a prolific inventor particularly in the development of light rays, embodying the science fiction invisible ray that was capable of destroying solid objects. On the right a pony and trap stands outside two local grocers/general store type shops, c1907

The Grove, where the owner is shown as a Mrs Matthews, a farmer; (probable family connections with the Matthews at Crossley Farm), is largely hidden in this view by the growing vegetation, which together with the foliage from the other side of the street creates a canopy under which the cameraman has set up his equipment to capture a peaceful scene of two young lads whose curiosity has taken them from their steeds, whilst one of our equine friends plods its weary way with a burdensome load, c1905

Mr Garrett has placed his camera to give us a much better view of the rank of cottages on the left now bathed in warm sunshine. Alex Jones shop and adjoining garage has expanded to include the serving of teas, as two young women head in that direction. One wonders what Mr Jones would make of the large filling station/shop that now dominates the area he once owned. A horse cart and carriage help to make this a most interesting and evocative picture, c1905

Our photographic journey has now brought us to the junction with Watley's End Road with its magnificent Elm Tree in the middle of the triangular area created by the layout of the roads. Without the aid of a dog, but possibly the help of a carter, and a well dressed lady on her bicycle, the shepherd is trying to get his flock to go in the right direction not helped by the position of the photographer; no wonder the sheep appear confused and are not sure which way to go, c1904.

The bright summer sunshine illuminates the front of *The Swan Inn* (landlady Mrs Eliza Pearce) as two cyclists, who have the freedom of the road pass by watched by a young lad pulling his homemade carrying box. Hidden by the tree is Crossley House ~ the then residence of John C Gradidge, ~ although the gate across the entrance can be clearly seen, whilst to the left of the tree stands Crossley Cottages, c1920

A slightly different angle but still a lovely sunny shot of Crossley Corner with a picket fence now delineating the triangle created by the road junction, whilst across the road a Bristol Tramways omnibus has stopped to let-off its passengers, To the left of the *Swan Inn* were originally two cottages, which were around 1890, amalgamated into one when the landlord created smoking concerts, providing his patrons with a clay pipe and as much tobacco they could smoke, c1904.

To take this picture, Mr Garrett has turned his glass-plate camera completely around so that he is looking back towards the village. The magnificent elm tree has been replaced with a new tree helping to open out the newly created grass area currently taken over by a small group of children enjoying the sunny weather. The general store in the background is now a solicitor's office, whilst the entrance to Crossley Farm (Jeffery Matthews) is on the extreme right, c1912

Crossley Farm House with possibly Jeffery Matthews and family, c 1907
Over the years milk from the farm was delivered the local inhabitants, possibly from the prize winning goats that were kept there

The village pond, Flaxpits Lane complete with a group of ducks, c1954. Almost certainly the name of the lane will have its origins back in the mid sixteenth century when Henry Vlll decreed that every parish should set aside an area of land for the sole purpose of growing flax.

The oarsman steadies the boat as the angler watches hopefully for a fish to bite, but a closer reference to all of the occupants of the boat, plus those on shore shows that this is a carefully staged picture composed by and for the benefit of the photographer, 1910

As stated on the card, this is a view of the fishponds at Winterbourne. Behind the camera is the early nineteenth century Barton Cottage at a time when the cottage was still sporting a thatched roof, c1910

Looking across the rooftops of the properties in Quarry Barton to the newly erected viaduct carrying the Great Western Railway's main line from London to S. Wales c1904 (see picture on page 64 of my book *Around Downend, Frenchay & Hambrook)*

Seen below is Winterbourne railway station opened in July 1903, it was constructed at the eastern end of the brick built viaduct that consists of eleven arches each with a 56 foot span, and each just under 93 feet high. At the time when this photograph was taken the station employees number eight, there were brick built offices/waiting rooms on both sides of the track with canopies linked by a covered footbridge, c1905

Somewhat taking his life in his hands, the photographer has set himself up with tripod and camera between the running lines to capture the section of track that not only ran through the station but also ran as straight as a die for well over a mile. Safely on the platform, staff members and well-dressed passengers watch on with interest, and possibly some anxiety whilst, behind the building on the left is the site of the Huckford Quarry, c1908.

With the camera position turned completely around from the view below, a down freight headed by ex GWR mixed traffic loco 6849 is caught running through all that remains of Winterbourne station, May 1964

Ex GWR pannier tank locomotive No.9769 takes a Railway Society special through Winterbourne station on its way towards Westerleigh, 26th September 1959

A somewhat narrow Church Road dips between substantial stone walls holding back the rough pastures of Church Farm the house of which can be clearly seen in the centre of the picture, whilst together with the tower of St Peter's the pump house chimney of the local waterworks dominate the skyline. A man in bowler hat, and two children watch with curiosity, c1904

Two similar but differently angled views of Church Farm, and Church Road with, on the right, the Brockeridge high ground in the background, note the smoke drifting from the chimney indicating that the West Gloucester Water Works Co were using their steam pump to extract around 250,000 gallons per day of drinking water from the old iron mines that would otherwise have gone to waste c1912 Below we are

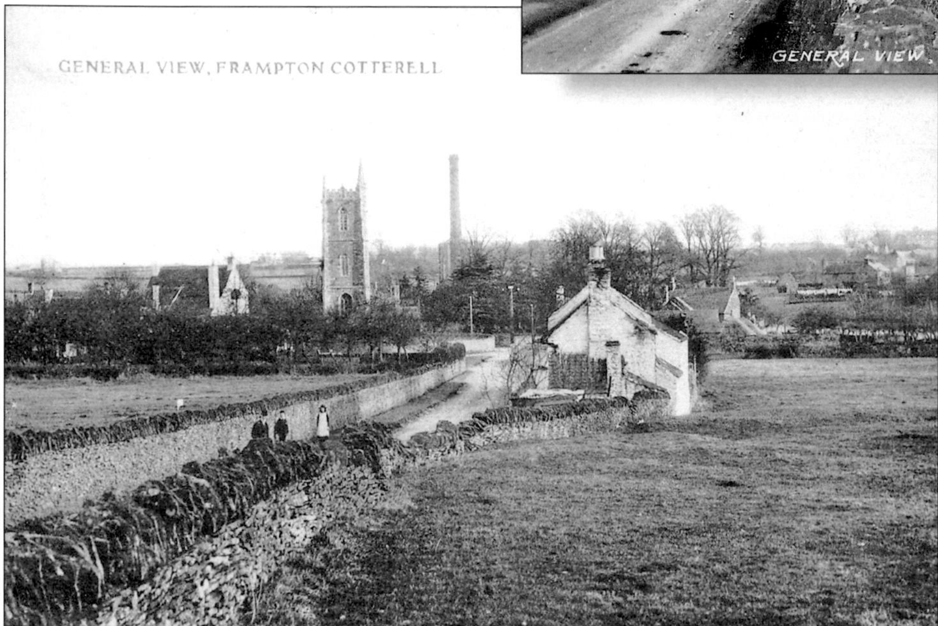

provided with a more frontal aspect of the farmhouse, as is the true width of Church Road. Both views enable today's reader to really appreciate how quiet and rural this area of Frampton Cotterell once was; particularly when compared with the same area today with its large housing estate spread-eagled over the pastures that once were there, and the roadway that had to be changed to accommodate the need to have our own personalised transport c1908

A close-up of the West Gloucester Water Works Company's pumping station constructed over what was in the 1860/70's the Red Gin Pit an iron ore mine however the ore became increasingly more and more difficult to extract, owing to the constant ingress if flood water and the mine was abandoned around 1878 with the site being taken over in the early 1880's In the middle of the picture is the tall redbrick structure that housed the pumping equipment, c1908

A quiet, peaceful and motor vehicle free view of Church Road, with just one pedestrian enjoying a lonesome stroll, c1954

Having struggled to carry his camera equipment up the spiral stairs within St Peter's tower, the cameraman was treated to this wonderful view that has been frozen in time of the Goose Green area that leads up to the adjourning neighbourhood of Brockeridge. Church Road as seen here was realigned in 1968, which would involve the destruction of the cottages in the foreground, c1952

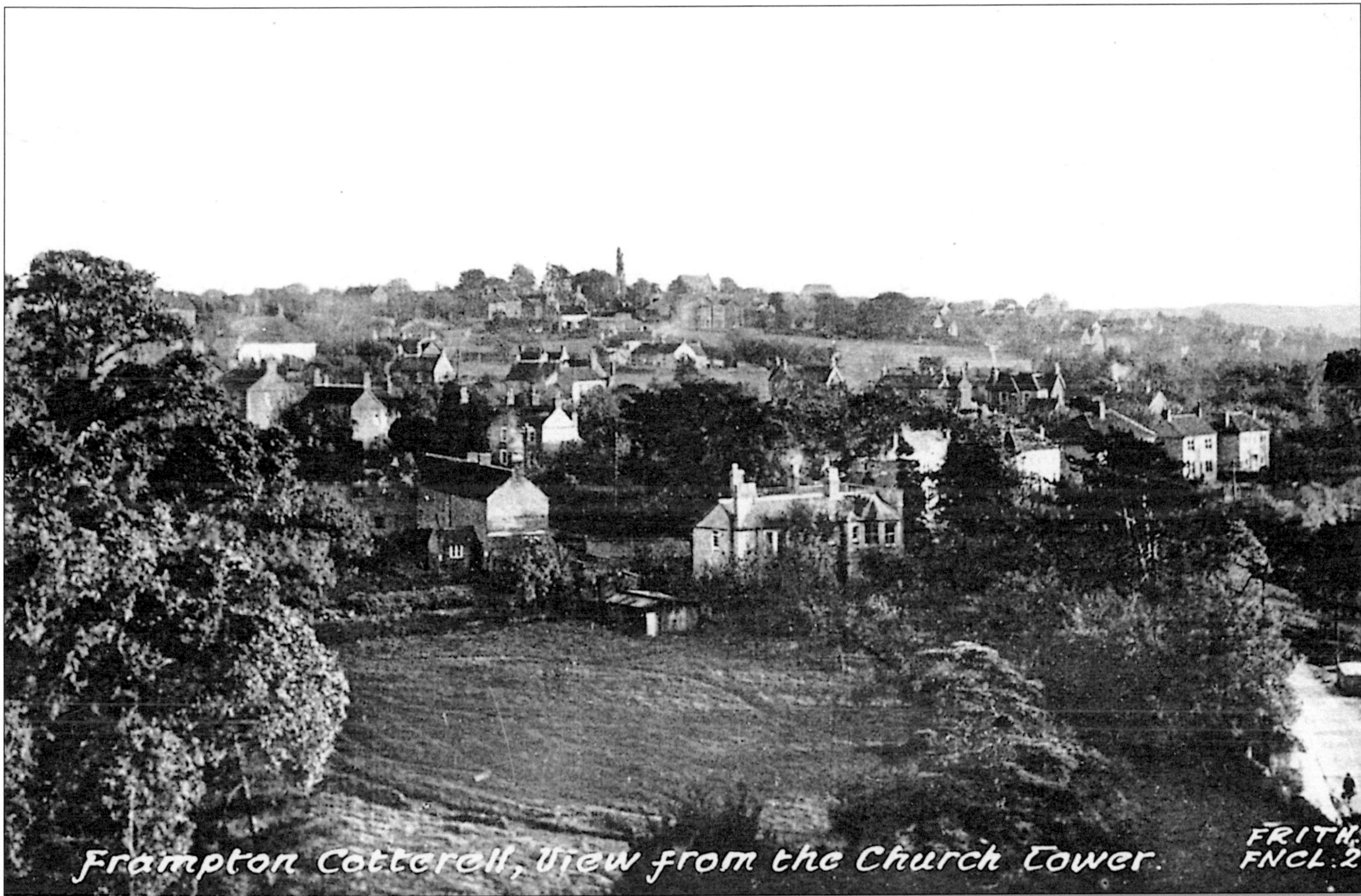

It is not known whether it was the same cameraman who had to climb St Peter's tower again to capture this different view of the Goose Green area of Frampton Cotterell, but many years after it was taken we are still able to study those subtle changes between this picture and the one on the previous page, whereas a comparison with today's views will unfortunately show changes far less subtle and not always for the better, c1960

Yet another view taken from the tower of St Peter's, this time showing in the foreground Park Lane, with in the mid distant *Step House,* and the local hostelry known as the *Live and Let Live.* Beyond are the new properties at the start of the road called Sunnyside, c1960

Two distinct bungalow styles can be clearly seen in this broad view of the newly constructed Benson's Estate. Built on land that was once part of Church Farm we are in this picture looking over Beaufort Road; Winchcombe Road and Foxe Road, c1964

Until around 1955, a view from St Peter's looking in the same direction would have been open fields on both sides of Church Road with a few isolated properties including Church Farm now demolished (see the pictures on page 31 showing the same view but in reverse). Now the field on the right already contains, behind the *Globe Inn,* new bungalows of Benson's Estate, and beyond these Belcher's Barton can be seen, c1961

The original village Post Office in Church Road was in use for most of the first four decades of the last century. Here the photographer has gathered together a group of smartly dressed your men from the village, all no doubt pleased, if a little curious, of the rare opportunity of having their picture taken, although the accompanying dog is less than interested in the antics of the cameraman In the doorway is the proprietor Mr G Colborn sporting grey whiskers and a top hat as he hopes that you will enter his emporium that sells drapery, groceries as well as postal matters, c1910.

Church Road with its row of magnificent elm trees shielding the tower of St Peter's church, c1907

The tower of St Peter's hides behind the tall and heavily foliaged elms that fringe Church Road, as an elderly gentleman takes his constitutional on a bright summer's day complete with a walking stick, and a top hat; note the well-cultivated garden on the left, c1914

This is a similar but different view of the same area of Church Road although the camera has been moved to the other side of the arched bridge, destroyed on the 18th December 1965 when twelve hours of heavy rain of almost one inch per hour caused the R Frome to burst its banks cutting the village into two requiring an emergency Bailey Bridge constructed by the army to connect the two halves. In this view the trees appear to be waking from their winter sleep and are about to burst into life, c1905

An early photographic picture looking down a rather muddy Church Road, with on the right a solitary little girl standing outside what appears to be a general store whilst in front of the gates stands a young boy, c1904.

The illustrations on this and the next page enable us in conjunction with the previous picture to track through time the progress of this part of Church Road, and in particular the shop business at the top of the hill.

Some eight years have passed before we reach the next photograph on the left, with little or nothing changed. The condition of the road is summer dust rather then winter mud, the shop is still a general store, and equine horsepower together with two or three bicycles appear to be the main means of transportation, c1912.

Much has happened between the taking of these two pictures, including a World War, with the threat of yet another one, a private motorcar (GHT 266) parks outside the shop that is now the village Post Office, A telephone box has arrived, as have Lyons Ice Creams, but the basic view remains the same, c1937

This is the last in the set of four pictures showing the small changes made to this particular part of Frampton Cotterell over a period of around fifty years. A mother and son stroll into the Post Office, whilst an elderly gentleman waits to cross the quiet and peaceful road, which although now tarmacked, has already been dug-up, c1955.

Newly constructed Winchcombe Road basks in the evening sun, with just one car occupying the roadway and no doubt the residents are indoors familiarizing themselves with their new surroundings c 1953.

Built during the second decade of the nineteenth century, the windmill on the right was 60ft high and equipped with rotating sails but by the mid 1850's the sails became redundant being replaced by a more efficient steam engine. It is believed that the girl is one of the Walter sisters who lived in the adjacent cottage, c1910

At the end of the sweeping drive on the left is, according to the caption, the Vicarage, but more often referred to as the Rectory, a name also given to the nearby road. When this picture was taken c1908 the Revd Thomas Belcher and his wife Mary were in occupation, and as a couple they allowed many church and village gatherings to be held in the extensive garden attached to the house, which was sadly demolished during the building of the large 1960's housing estates.

Route 26 Bristol (Tramway Centre) to Frampton Cotterell (Church Road) at Frampton on the 20th October 1913. AE 3187 a Bristol built C60 type chassis

With St Peter's church acting as a background we are able to absorb the rural setting of Frampton Cottrell as we look across the water meadows with the gentle River Frome meandering its way under an ancient arched bridge on its way to meet the River Avon in Bristol, c1910

At the turn of the last century speculative builders considered Frampton Cotterell to be an ideal county area for the construction of upper class villas, and built these Edwardian style properties along a new road to be named after "Clyde of India", although exactly what Baron Clyde had to do with Frampton and its surroundings has never been explained, perhaps it just sounded posh, c1908

For around fifty years between 1818 and 1869 Frampton Cotterell was a local centre for the manufacture of felt and fur hats resulting in the construction of the three-storey building seen here in Park Lane. Such was the demand that by around 1835 there were over 100 employees each producing at least a dozen hats per week although the amount of dust and fibres in the air caused serious long-term lung problems, closed by the turn of the century the properties are now homes, c1911

Although one or two bandsmen appear to have grown out of their trousers, the proud men of the Hambrook Brass Band are about to lead off the village procession in celebration of King George V's coronation in 1911. Note the Boy Scouts with their staffs lined up behind outside of *Skinner's Yard* and the overhead bunting and Union Jack flags.

The band has played the stirring tunes; the celebration procession has passed, and now is the time for the girls to entertain the crowd with a skipping race, no shorts or trousers for these young ladies who also had to keep a high level of decorum as they skipped and ran, 1911

The *Rising Sun* in Ryecroft Road built around 1850, and converted into a free public house by the Howes family during the 1860's. This family had a long association with this pub with Frederick Howes recorded as a beer retailer and butcher at this address in 1905.Not many years afterwards the pub was acquired by Bristol United Breweries, and became a tied house, with tenant Gilbert Bisp landlord. When this picture was taken the brewery firm Courage were the owners, c1955

Alfred Edward Henry Drew, of The Chestnuts, Frampton common; was not only an agent for Walter A. Wood Harvesting Machines; he was also a manufacturer of agricultural implements, and a carriage builder. In his private (non business) life he was the organist of the local parish church, as well as being a teacher of music, c1905.

Perrinpit Farm, Perrinpit Road, Nr North Corner, Frampton Cotterell, c1912

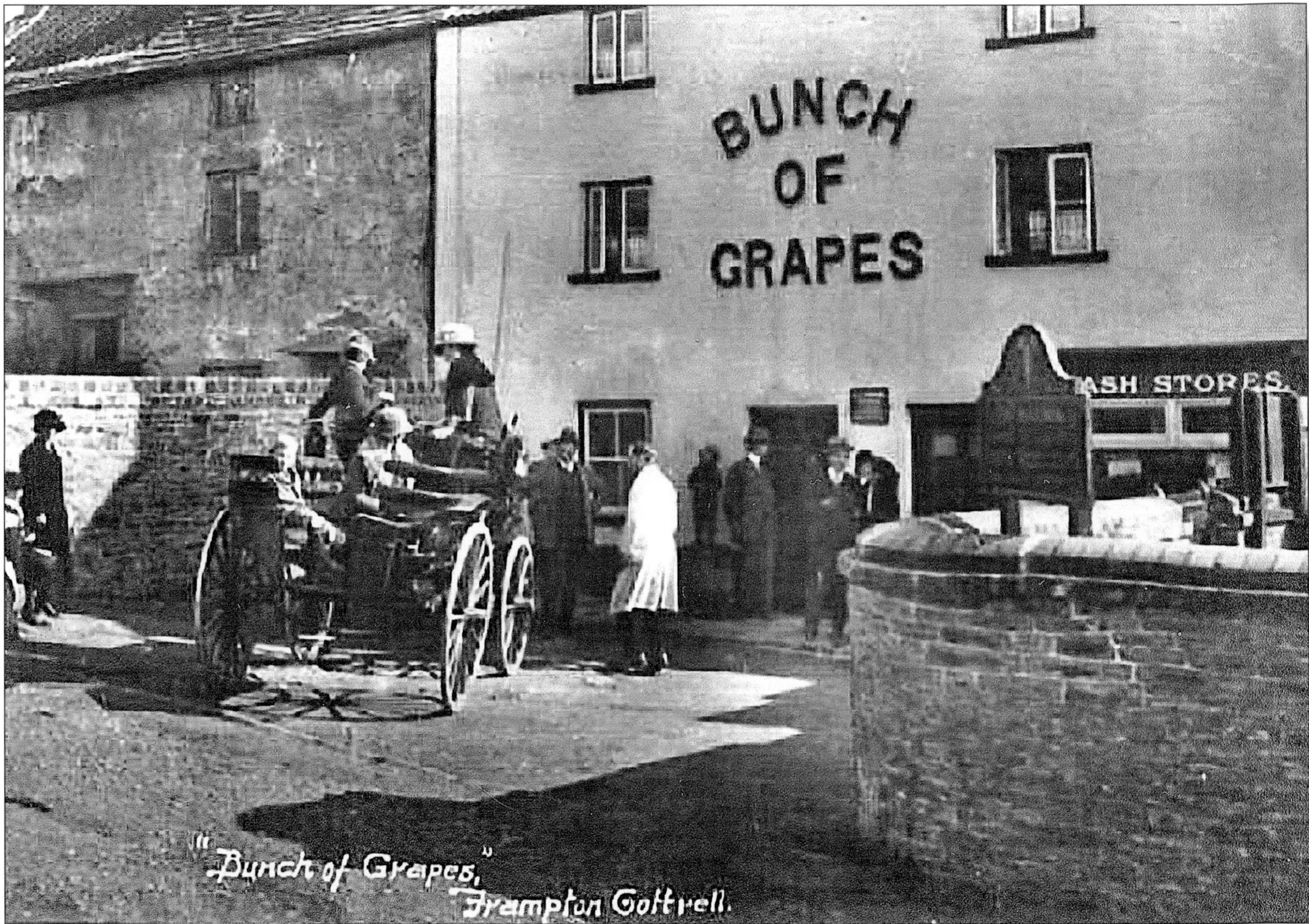

People gather outside the *Bunch of Grapes* in Woodend Road for a possible if uncomfortable trip into Bristol but at least it will start in bright sunshine. To the right is Zion Chapel; whilst to the left is a rather derelict house, c1912.

The Mill Pond and surrounding countryside creates its own sylvan atmosphere that was no doubt enjoyed by many at the end of the last century. Interestingly the card was used as a birthday card and contained the following message *Ivy and I have been laid (sic) by the millpond trying to get sunburnt, but we hav'nt yet, c1904*

Children look over the stone wall that borders Church Road, whilst behind them is the Wesleyan Chapel, with to the left the Country Stores. With a strong nucleus of Wesleyans amongst the evangelists in the village, the chapel was built in 1821 by the former, and lasted through to 2000, c1910.

The sylvan setting that was once the image of Frampton Cotterell, as we step back in time and gaze down Goose Green, past the solitary cottage on the right, and small paddocks on the left to reach the houses in Clyde Road, and St Peter's tower pointing to the sky with a complete backdrop of open fields, c1926

Bristol Road on its way to Iron Acton as it approached the North Corner junction with the *Cross Hands Inn,* advertising Georges Bristol Beers, and Perrinpit Road on the left On the right Church Road takes us back to the heart of Frampton Cotterell passing an old cottage and a motor vehicle repair garage c1926.

On the right is the frontage of the *Cross Hands Inn* as we are invited to look back along Bristol Road past the tall and imposing Elm Trees. Built around 1825 it was modernised in the mid 1970's and given the rather grandiose name of the *Western Coach House* bearing in mind that it never was a coach house. However its new name did not enhance its ability to attract new trade, and the inn closed in 2006, being converted to residential dwellings and in doing so it perhaps went back to its original purpose, c1904

On the edge and to the north of Iron Acton is *Mudgedown Farm* as seen on the left. Note lady in white dress sitting under the "Monkey Puzzle" tree, whilst a gentleman, possibly Frederick George Smith, sits under the left-hand window. A picture by the well know local photographer Murray Dowding of around 1911.

Another Murray Dowding picture this time of Mrs Nell's hounds, watched by a number of locals including one on a bike, which is believed to have been taken in the grounds of *Mudgedown Farm,* c1911

A view of the frontage of the substantial Hill House, once owned by Edward John Rose, c1905.

On the right is the attractive gateway, to Acton Court constructed; it is believed, during the 1680/90's when the main house in the background was being greatly altered, c1906

Two side elevation views of Acton Court, a restored Tudor Manor House, modified around 1528 with an addition of an east wing to Nicholas Poyntz's existing moated house. It is understood that this wing was extensively and sumptuously decorated with no expense spared so that the Poyntz's family could increase their position in Court by inviting and hopefully impressing Henry VIII and his wife Anne Boleyn to spend the night there, during the Royal couples tour of the West Country in 1535.However they were not the first royal couple to visit the Court as in 1486 Henry VII and his new bride Elizabeth slept there, after dining with Sir Robert Poyntz, who had been knighted by the king on Bosworth Field.

It is believed that during the 1580's Sir Walter Raleigh visited Acton Court not long after he returned from ventures in the New World with a collection of dried leaves called tobacco, and that the court possibly became the first house in the United Kingdom where tobacco was smoked.

Both pictures c1910

The pupils of the Church of England School have been brought to the boundary wall for a collective photograph, with their school in the background, no worry about health and safety in those days children were assumed to have a level of common sense and did not need to be wrapped in cotton wool, c1926

The junction of Wotton Road and Nibley Lane, with the village school and *Inglenook Cottage.* Although this picturess card appears to be a very iconic view of a country cottage and English Garden, closer look will show rising from the ground are two Shell petrolium globes and various accoutrements confirming that this is also an early form of filling station for the sale of petrol with the fuel pipes capable of being swung out over the pavement to feed the ever growing demand for liquid fuel. No forecourt instead you could remain in your car, press the horn and someone would come running to serve you, c1952

A view across the meadow and adjoining hedges from Holly Hill with East View cottages, to the left, and the junction of the High street and Wotton Road to the right, c1906

St James the Less, with its rare and exceptional cross, built on behalf of Sir Robert Poyntz in 1390 in memory of his late grandmother. Constructed on three steps with four buttresses, with the four sides intricately carved, caped by a pinnacled canopy. Although now showing its age, there is within the structure a ledge to rest a book, and from time to time the cross has been used as a preaching pulpit, c1904

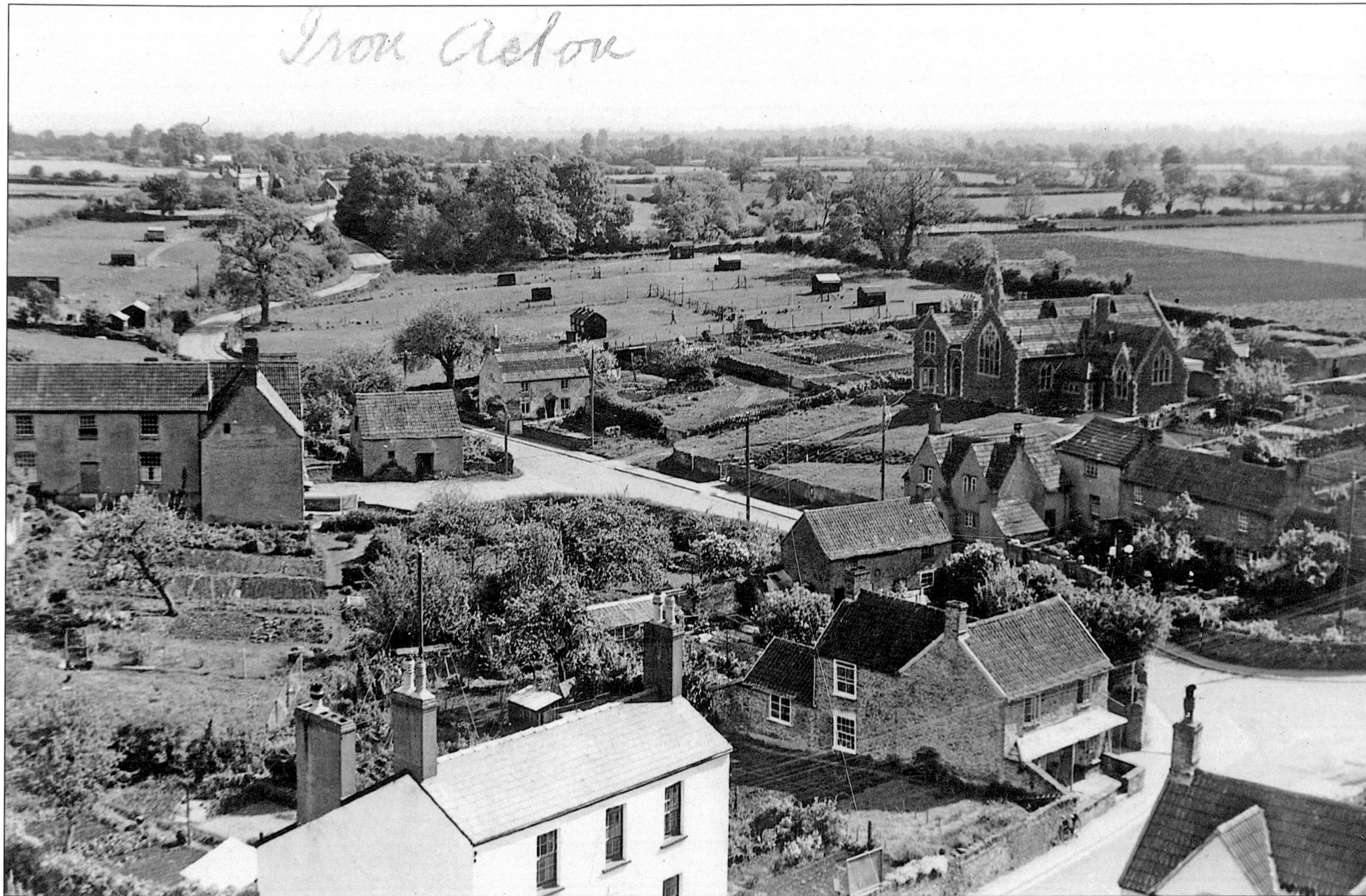

The eastern approach to the village as seen from the church tower, with *The Lamb Inn* and its long forecourt leading to Wotton Road, the Church of England School, and *The Nook.* On the right foreground is the junction with High Street, the Corner Shop *Church Cottage* and the Police Station; in addition it is also possible to make out the Shell globe petrol pumps in the grounds of *Inglenook Cottage,* c1950

The church yard, and cross with, on the right the ancient porch that contains a splendid old wooden door plus some sculptured stone that may well be Saxon in origin. The Church was probably constructed during the twelfth century being rebuilt at the expense of Sir Robert Poyntz at the same time the Cross-was being built, although at that stage the tower did not exist as this was not erected until 1490, c1910

At the time that this picture was taken the art of photography was still a source of curiosity, whilst at the same time it was perfectly safe to stand in the middle of High Street to consider or try to understand exactly what was going on. As for the young lady her curiosity is not that strong, and wisely stays close to the wall just in case she needs to retreat behind the wall, c1907

The police station, and corner shop with its enamel adverts for cigarettes and tea an interesting view believed to have been taken in the early 1920's when the shop proprietor was George Wollen who, according to the directory of the time, was also the gardener to the Rev. George R Browne MA, c1921

This image of school children on their way home has been frozen in time, as the photographer makes use of the summer sunshine as it highlights Dean Lodge on the left, whilst the dominant tower of St James the Less rises majestically above the village, c1960

Two separate and interesting views looking back along the High Street towards the church, on the left a card published by Miss Elizabeth Fugill c1908 the sub postmistress at Latteridge, and on the right a card that was published c1903.

The *Crown Inn c1923* (proprietor William Allen King) dominates this part of the High Street. Closed around 2005 the property has now been converted into a private house. Prior to the First World War during the tenancy of Mrs Blanchard the inn was known as the *Rose & Crown* but appears to have had its name shortened to the *Crown Inn* throughout much of its existence. Reference to local registers shows the *Rose & Crown* name was in use during the period immediately prior to the First World War, but there is no photographic evidence to support the registers.

The camera has been moved back up along the High Street and turned completely around to enable us to look towards the west, as the summer shadows almost reach across the road, c1917 Once again the sign still only shows the name "*Crown Inn*"

The High Street looking east towards the church, c1907

George Fursman's grocery shop, with a pair of two wheeled farm carts, with their complementary horses, dogs and drivers positioned to create an atmospheric image now frozen in time so that subsequent generations have the opportunity of looking back to a time long gone, c1910

The photographer has stopped the new fangled automobile with its passengers, and gathered together a large group of village children to animate what would otherwise be a dull picture. In the background is *The Boot House; Primrose Cottage* and *The Old Saddlers* although none of these name may have been in use at the time of the picture, c1912

A short walk along Park Street brings us to the large village Green. With the Congregational Chapel on the left, the photographer appears to have interrupted the work of replacing soil and re-seeding the nearest part of the Green, with the workmen spread around to create this absorbing picture of c1908

From winter we move to summer for this similar picture of the village green. A pony and trap has been captured by the camera, as have two grazing ponies, plus a sense of peace when the then pace of life gave our ancestors a level of contentment perhaps not fully understood or appreciated today, c1907.

Part of the Village Green with on the right behind the lady and gentleman is the junction with Park Street that leads back to the High Street. In the background the buildings left to right are *Penny Farthing Cottage; Green Cottage* and *Rustic Cottage, c1907*

Muddy roads and pathways criss-cross the Green, as the photographer has captured this moist winter scene that includes a bevy of village children one of whom is in charge of a coach perambulator; and behind her it is possible to make out the row of cottages that run along the B4059, c1904

From the village green we have returned to the High Street as we look back to the junction with Park Street and two young girls in their pinafore dresses as they stand outside one of the many small shops since converted into dwellings and now known as *The Glove Hitch,* but which then was a boot & shoe shop belonging to Miss Hester Mainstone. Note the inn on the right is still only called *Crown Inn,* c1905

With the camera pulled back, and many years passed since the previous picture was taken we look back as the High Street bends to the left past a small shop/café as a young woman stands in the sunshine on what is otherwise a very quiet and peaceful village with little or no traffic to disturb the harmony of the surroundings, c1954

With the camera turned completely around we are again afforded the opportunity of being taken back in time to study the High Street as it leads our gaze towards the *White Hart* in the background. On the left is *Trent House*; whilst beyond in the next building Charles Pullin was a cycle agent. A mother and daughter plus two little girls pose to have their pictures taken, perhaps for the first time in their lives. Posted on the 24th December 1904 as a Christmas card, with the sender absolutely confident that the card would be delivered the next day in Dursley.

The sun shine's brightly and highlights *Laburnum House* with its shell porch as a gentleman checks to see what is going on, whilst further along the High Street a horse waits patiently as his driver makes the required deliveries, c1908

A bevy of young villagers, together with a variety of wheeled vehicles have been assembled by the photographer outside of *Trent House* at the end of the High Street close to its junction with Latteridge Road. The building in the background is the *White Hart* ~ Philip Sutcliffe Sunderland publican, c1908

The triangular turnpike as you approach Iron Acton along the Bristol Road from Frampton Cotterell and join Station Road with, on the left *Turnpike House* the tower of St Peter's Church and *Wisteria Cottage* in the middle. Sent to London as a birthday card 2nd October 1924

The Station and level crossing whilst in the background the Bristol Road over bridge can be seen. The branch line that in 1872 terminated at Thornbury was built in 1868 to tap into the local wealth of coal, iron and quarried stone, and just the other side of the gate the line that originally branched off to Frampton Cottrell can be seen as it went under the loading gauge. In 1875 the line to Frampton was closed and the truncated line was used as a coal siding. Closed to passengers in 1944, having been used during the War to convey wounded soldiers to a hospital in Thornbury, the whole line was closed in 1967, picture c1950

With the level crossing gates closed by the train guard ex LMS 44553 waits to take its mixed freight train through a very dilapidated Iron Acton station on its way to Yate junction during the 15th March 1962; on the left of the engine was the coal siding. Despite the poor level of maintenance, the line would remain open for a further five years when it stood derelict for fifteen years until rail from the Mangotsfield to Bath branch was used to re-open the track to the quarry at Tytherington.

Two separate but slightly different views looking down along Station Road also known as Mill Lane towards the stone bridge over the River Frome. With both views they show left to right the old cottage and the old mill of Algars Manor that was originally built during the sixteenth century.

The way in which the two little girls are holding hands could mean that they are sisters, with the taller girl carrying a small basket of flowers. c1924

Identified by the photographer as Mill Lane, the old mill and adjourning cottage have been captured by his art to reflect the ambience of the rural setting and the summer sunshine, c1910.

A gentleman sits on the parapet of the Old Mill Stream with a background of dense summer foliage. Picture taken by G G Willson of Iron Acton, c1905